"*I*
sou

Lord Jesus, even Jesus
the Word. Everything I set my hand
to is successful today. I cannot be
conquered; I cannot be defeated. I am a
stranger to failure. For me to fail, God
would have to fail, and God cannot
fail. The Greater One dwells in me, and
He puts me over. I have His abilities.
That is what I have, and that
is who I am."

When I was about 5 years old, I started saying the above confession over myself every day. I believe that making a life-long habit of confessing the Word and other scripture-inspired quotes every day is the reason for my prosperity today.

Chantell M. Cooley, Author

STAND ON THE WORD

CONFESSIONS AND MEDITATIONS OF A CHRISTIAN LEADER

CHANTELL M. COOLEY

Published by:
Cooley Communications
21982 University Lane
Orange Beach, AL 36561

Copyright 2016, Chantell Cooley

ISBN #978-0-9976907-6-7 (paperback)
ISBN #978-0-9976907-8-1 (ebook)

Cover Design: Brittany Armistead

Editors:

Michelle Ofori-Ansah, Founder
Primedoor Media and Marketing
Dallas, TX
www.PrimeDoor.org

Solomon Ofori-Ansah, Founder and President
Isosports International, Inc.
Dallas, TX
www.IsoSoccer.com

DEDICATION

To Mimi, my mother, who left me a great legacy of meditating on the Word. She and I confessed scriptures together all my life. I owe my success and this book to her influence. Thank you Mom!

TABLE OF CONTENTS

GLOSSARY OF CONFESSIONS

FOREWORD

Next to knowing Jesus as my Lord and personal Savior, perhaps my greatest discovery is getting to know and appreciate His voice. For over 40 years, meditating on the Word of God has sustained me in my personal life as well as ministry. But beyond sustenance, I have thrived where others have failed or given up. As one of the pioneering women at the frontlines of ministry, I have traveled to and ministered in over 130 countries and broken through some of the toughest terrains for the Gospel. I can testify that all of the success I have enjoyed is because of the Word.

In this book, Chantell Cooley, my spiritual daughter who is also a very succcessful entrepreneur and businesswoman, demystifies scriptural meditation and gives you the one key you need to be successful. In easy-to-read, everyday English, Chantell expounds on the power of the Word of God, the benefits of scriptural meditation, and most importantly, she teaches you how to meditate on the Word.

Also, Chantell shares with the reader some of her lifelong favorite scriptures and confessions that have been the cornerstone of her success. If you are Christian caught in cycles of poverty and stagnation, you will find the answer to your progress in this book.

The Bible is for all who hunger and thirst. Its message will uplift anyone who dares to believe and put it into practice. I have experienced the power and benefit of meditating on the Scriptures firsthand, as well as having seen it liberate individual destinies, families and people groups from the ravages of sin, sickness and poverty. I want to encourage you to take the message of this book very seriously. Make an effort to develop the daily discipline of meditating on and confessing scripture, and you will experience life-giving, refreshing and transforming power in every area of your life.

Dr. Marilyn Hickey
President and Founder
Marilyn Hickey Ministries

AUTHOR'S NOTE

How do we get to the next level or become successful in life? This question plagues all of us to a different extent. Sometimes we look at the lives of people of great wealth or achievement and wonder how they did it. How did they get to be so successful? Is there a silver bullet? What is the magic formula to success?

I believe that Joshua may also have struggled with this same question. It is fair to say that Joshua was already successful by the time he took over from Moses. He was an accomplished military commander, well-known in Israel and neighboring nations, mightily used of God during Israel's toughest times, and well-trained and equipped to be the next leader. But after the death of Moses, as he took over leadership of Israel, he too began to wonder how he would fit into those huge shoes of Moses and ultimately become successful at his new position. With the change, he began to feel the weight and stress of leadership.

As Joshua wondered, the Word of the Lord came to him:

"Keep this Book of the Law always on your lips; meditate on it day and night, so that you may be careful to do everything written in it. Then you will be prosperous and successful." Joshua 1:8

The answer to Joshua's worries and concerns was really very simple. All he had to do was meditate on the Scriptures day and night, walk in obedience, and success would be his. And most importantly, it was within his reach. It was not esoteric or mystical; it was very practical. Joshua was capable of executing it right from the comfort of his bedroom. Was that really it? Was it really that simple?

As it was for Joshua, so it is for us. I am living proof that this scripture, Joshua 1:8, works. When I was 17 years old, I began studying the Bible. I began to find verses that were applicable to my life and meditate on them. I would read and repeat them to myself and to my family. I also began to read a chapter of Proverbs daily, so that I was able to read through the entire book of Proverbs every month. Over time, I began to see the results.

If you have read my story, you know that my family struggled to achieve success. One of the things that helped to break the cycle of poverty was the Word. During very hard times, the Word would give me hope. It kept me laughing when there was no reason to laugh, and it kept me dreaming when there was no reason to believe.

As my family spoke the Word over our lives, things began to change. My dad got a job which would later lead him to the founding of our university. We came out of miserable debt and began to prosper in every area of our lives. We went from not having any food in the house to having a home we owned and solid jobs.

I met my husband by speaking the Word over my life and praying for God to lead my steps. Meditating on the Word is the reason I am who I am today and I am where I am in life. Success follows me wherever I go, because the

Word is always working for me. It will set you up for success as well. The Word will pull you out of debt, fix a bad marriage and heal your body, if you allow it to.

I am so amazed at how my life has changed, and I want to share that with you. I want to help you stay on the right path and go deeper with God. I want you to experience success in all areas of your life, moving up the ladder in your job or being successful in ministry or the area of your calling. I invite you to join me in exploring the power and the blessing of meditating on the Word.

INTRODUCTION

"If you want to grow, read your Bible and pray every day." These are the words of a popular Sunday School song. The truth of that song is as relevant today as it was when I learned it as a child. Having a daily devotional time helps us to get to know the Word and to develop faith for our Christian walk.

And there is more. To achieve success in life, it is not enough to have head knowledge of the Bible and be morally upright. The Word of God must dwell in us richly (Col 3:16); it must be near us, even in our mouth and in our hearts (Rom 10:8). The Word must enter our psyche and the very depths of our spirit. We must be full of the Word. The only way to achieve that is through daily scriptural meditation.

This book will help you to meditate on the Word of God on a daily basis. I will start you off with some of my favorite scriptures that I have meditated on daily for as long as I can remember. As you do it faithfully, you will begin to see the power of the Word of God manifest in your life. Success will follow naturally.

CHAPTER 1
THE POWER OF THE WORD

How do you view the words of the Bible? Do you consider them to be history, poetry or prophecy? The way you see the Bible is very important. For you to make the Word a part of your daily routine and reap its benefits, you must first appreciate its power. Let us review a few scriptures that speak to the power of the Word.

"For the Word of God is alive and active. Sharper than any double-edged sword, it penetrates even to dividing soul and spirit, joints and marrow; it judges the thoughts and attitudes of the heart."
Hebrews 4:12

According to this scripture, the Word is immensely powerful, with more than laser-sharp capabilities. It is able to enter places in our lives that cannot be touched by the surgeon's scapel or the counselor's advice, far beyond what motivational speakers or life coaches can speak to. The Word is able to transcend the natural into the supernatural realm, giving the Holy Spirit access to the very depths of your heart and soul.

How often do you ask God about the next step for your life? How many times have you asked God to make your life purpose clear? The Word can enter the thoughts and intents of your heart and shine a light on your life's purpose and heart's desires, bringing insight and revelation into these important questions.

"For I am not ashamed of the gospel, because it is the power of God that brings salvation to everyone who believes: first to the Jew, then to the Gentile." Romans 1:16

The gospel is God's instrument of deliverance and salvation. For those who believe it, the Word of God has the power to change their lives regardless of their ancestry, ethnicity or cultural roots. If you dare to believe, you will experience continuous transformation. Most people believe the Word and they get saved, but after that, they don't follow through and believe for the Word of God to change and impact every aspect of their lives.

"All Scripture is God-breathed and is useful for teaching, rebuking, correcting and training in righteousness." 2 Timothy 3:16

Yes, the Bible has stories about ordinary people like you and I, as well as some very great and very spiritual ones. It also has deep prophetic literature, such as Isaiah, and some wisdom literature, such as Proverbs. However, every bit of it is the Inspired Living Word of God. No matter where you are in your life journey, you can use the Word to guide you. And irrespective of what you are going through, you can count on its power to save and deliver you.

The Word Gives You Power Over Evil

In the account of the temptation of Jesus in Matthew 4, we see His complete reliance on the Scriptures to defeat His foe. The Lord's response to the first temptation was:

"Jesus answered, 'It is written: Man shall not live on bread alone, but on every word that comes from the mouth of God.'" Matthew 4:4

Satan did not relent; he persisted with a second temptation, this time quoting a scripture to validate the temptation.

"'If You are the Son of God,' he said, 'throw Yourself down. For it is written: He will command His angels concerning You, and they will lift You up in their hands, so that You will not strike Your foot against a stone.'"
Matthew 4:6

Again the Lord, weakened in the flesh by a 40-day fast, countered with a scripture:

"Jesus answered him, 'It is also written: Do not put the Lord your God to the test.'"
Matthew 4:7

Satan's final attempt was also resisted with a scripture:

"Jesus said to him, 'Away from me, Satan! For it is written: Worship the Lord your God, and serve Him only.'" Matthew 4:10

The power of the Word cannot be overemphasized. That is how Jesus overcame the enemy—by confessing the Word. He responded to each of the temptations with "it is written…" making a reference to and quoting the scriptures three times. But beyond knowing and confessing scripture appropriately, Jesus also understood the deeper meanings found in the Bible. When Satan also quoted a scripture to support the second temptation, Jesus was able to respond biblically with sound interpretation of the Word and was not deceived by Satan's deliberate misappropriation of scripture.

So it's good to make a habit of reading and memorizing scriptures, but striving to understand the Word is crucial. It can make the difference between failure and success and between a victorious and vibrant Christian life and a struggling faith walk. The more you meditate on the Scriptures, the better you understand them and are able to apply them correctly and effectively in a situation.

The Benefits of the Word

"The Lord directs the steps of the godly. He delights in every detail of their lives."
Psalm 37:23 (NLT)

The Word will change your life. Remember that the Lord directs our steps, and He is in every detail of our lives. If you are wondering what your purpose is or what your next step in life is, turn to the Word. It will make a way for you and open doors for you. The Word keeps you on the right path so you don't get sidetracked with the stresses of life. The Word keeps you attentive spiritually and open to hearing the voice of Holy Spirit.

If you are a leader in the marketplace, reading the Bible will help you make decisions that are virtuous and just with your business and its employees. And it will give you wisdom to make plans that will impact your productivity and help you advance your career. If you work in the ministry, reading the Bible and truly digging into the Word will allow you to help those you are teaching and guiding.

If you are a stay-at-home parent, meditating on the scriptures will help you lead your children and family and keep you safe. My mom, Mimi, was a stay-at-home mom, and she made a point to say Bible verses and pray over us everyday.

If you are a young person, not out in the world yet but preparing yourself for it, I encourage you to meditate on the Word now, in preparation for your family one day. The Word will take you to new levels and open doors for you at a very young age.

The Word can also be a warning to get you out of situations that could set you up for failure. This next story shows how God uses the Word to keep us out of harm.

During my senior year in high school, my third period art class had one particular classmate who didn't like me. Every day he would taunt me over and over. He would question my beliefs and challenge me on why I believed in God, and I would reply with Bible verses. He would really get under my skin, but

I knew that I had to keep my cool and just give him the Word. This guy would put notes with demonic symbols in my locker and try to get inside my head. Between classes or on breaks, I would go to my locker for my books, and I would find these round demonic symbols just sitting on top of my books. He had slipped them through the vents in the front of the locker.

Another time I was walking to my car after school, and during the day someone had slit my tires. I knew it was this same guy, trying to make me waiver from my beliefs, but all this did was inspire me to be more on fire for God. You see, when the heat starts getting turned up in your life, you know you are doing something right. The devil won't mess with people who are not making a difference. He goes after those who are living on the edge with God and being used by Him to change lives.

During this season, there were times that fear would literally come over me, but God kept me safe through all this. The Word was in me and through me and nothing by any means could hurt me (Luke 10:19). The strength of the Word keeps you safe. Psalm 91 is a great chapter that talks about safety. Having these scriptures memorized has kept me protected in many situations. You can start memorizing them right now, and start reaping the benefits in your life. If you are by yourself, I recommend that you read them aloud.

Psalm 91

Whoever dwells in the shelter of the Most High will rest in the shadow of the Almighty. I will say of the LORD, "He is my refuge and my fortress, my God, in whom I trust." Surely He will save you from the fowler's snare and from the deadly pestilence. He will cover you with His feathers, and under His wings you will find refuge; His faithfulness will be your shield and rampart.

You will not fear the terror of night, nor the arrow that flies by day, nor the pestilence that stalks in the darkness, nor the plague that destroys at midday. A thousand may fall at your side, ten thousand at your right hand, but it will not come near you. You will only observe with your eyes and see the punishment of the wicked.

If you say, "The LORD is my refuge," and you make the Most High your dwelling, no harm will overtake you, no disaster will come near your tent. For He will command His angels concerning you to guard you in all your ways; they will lift you up in their hands, so that you will not strike your foot against a stone.

You will tread on the lion and the cobra; you will trample the great lion and the serpent. "Because he loves Me," says the LORD, "I will rescue him; I will protect him, for he acknowledges My name. He will call on Me, and I will answer him; I will be with him in trouble, I will deliver him

and honor him.
With long life I will satisfy him and
show him My salvation."

CHAPTER 2
MEDITATION:
JOSHUA'S SUCCESS FORMULA

I can never emphasize it enough. If I could attribute my success and perseverance throughout my career to one personal habit, it would be meditating on the Word as often as I can. Taking time to meditate on the Word is so valuable and powerful. It took my family out of extreme poverty and a cycle of failure into a life of success.

By all means, learn all you can about how to get to the next level. Read as many self-help books and listen to as many motivational speakers as you can. I strongly recommend doing that, and I do so myself often. However, none can match the power of meditating on the Word of God. Without the Word in you, none of those efforts will amount to much. Yes, they can bring you money, fame or even success, but if you want Good Success, there is only one pathway to it: meditating on the Scriptures.

Let's take a look at Joshua 1:8 to see the kind of success God wants for you.

"Keep this Book of the Law always on your lips; meditate on it day and night, so that you may be careful to do everything written in it. Then you will be prosperous and successful."
Joshua 1:8

I love to dissect scriptures. I think that if you learn how to do this, it makes the Bible become real to you, in a personal way. You start desiring more of it once you understand it better. Let's begin to dissect Joshua 1:8.

1. Keep this Book of the Law always on your lips.

We must first understand what the "Book of the Law" means. To Joshua, the "Book of the Law" included the first five books of our Bible, written by Moses: Genesis, Exodus, Leviticus, Numbers and Deuteronomy. However, for us as we read the Bible today, it refers to the entire Bible from Genesis to Revelation.

Keeping the "Book of the Law" always on your lips means that you make a point to read it, to speak it and to pray it. That is why we confess the Word. The Word should be reflected in your language use and conversation. You must choose your words carefully. What you say should be positive, up-lifting and a blessing to others.

"Do not let any unwholesome talk come out of your mouths, but only what is helpful for building others up according to their needs, that it may benefit those who listen."
Ephesians 4:29

The only way to build others up is by using words inspired by and based on the Word of God.

"The tongue has the power of life and death, and those who love it will eat its fruit."
Proverbs 18:21

Not only are our words supposed to build others up, they are also to build ourselves up. When we use negative words to describe or categorize ourselves, they have a negative impact on our lives. They can demoralize us, kill our vision and dry up our sense of initiave. To be successful, you must constantly speak positive, life-giving words over yourself and into your situation, regardless of the circumstances. Then you can reap the fruit that comes from scripture-inspired confessions.

So how do we get to the point where the Word stays in our mouth, and our language is continuously edifying us and others, bearing the fruit of abundant life, inspiration and success?

"A good man brings good things out of the good stored up in his heart, and an evil man brings evil things out of the evil stored up in his heart. For the mouth speaks what the heart is full of." Luke 6:45

The answer is to fill our hearts with the Word of God, and that is where meditation comes in. Continuous scriptural meditation is the only tool we have to transport and translate the Word from the pages of the Bible into our lives, giving us power in our hearts and minds.

2. But you shall mediate on it...

Now, to meditate means to think upon, ponder and review daily. Another way to meditate is to memorize verses and be able to recall them from memory.

You should fill your thoughts with the Word of God. When we meditate on the Word, we think about it's meaning and how it applies to us and our situation.

As you meditate, you will begin to get insight into the Scriptures, sometimes even things you have never heard in a sermon. At times, another verse will come to mind and shed light on a particular scripture verse you are meditating on.

The Bible says that Mary, the mother of Jesus, would ponder over some of the prophecies that she received about Jesus. As a young mother, Mary didn't understand all of them and how they would all work out, but she meditated on them.

"But Mary treasured up all these things and pondered them in her heart." Luke 2:19

If you have a vision that God has placed in your heart or if you feel that you are called to do something, but you are not sure how it will all come to pass, it is okay. You first have to treasure that vision in your heart, like Mary did. Put value on it, and then continuously think on it and pray about it. You must meditate on the visions and dreams that God has placed on your heart. As you do so, you move from not being sure how you are going to accomplish them, to believing they are possible, and eventually you begin to see yourself being able to fulfill them.

When we meditate on the Word, it reflects in the quality of our thoughts.

"Finally, brothers and sisters, whatever is true, whatever is noble, whatever is right, whatever is pure, whatever is lovely, whatever is admirable— if anything is excellent or praiseworthy—think about such things." Philippians 4:8

Beyond quality, quantity also matters. God wants us thinking about the Word often.

3. But you shall mediate on it day and night.

Did God say to meditate once a week? Twice a week? Once a month? No, He said to meditate or ponder the Word day and night. That means that not a day goes by without you reading your Bible or meditating on the Scriptures. The Word of God is your lifeline; it is what sustains the believer spiritually and manifests in a life of success. So you must make a point to develop this discipline and include meditating on the Word in your daily routine. You should occupy your thoughts with the Word on a daily and nightly basis, thinking about various verses and stories in the Bible.

4. So that you may be careful to do everything written in it.

Because of the power of the Word of God, meditating on the Word is inherently powerful, and it releases enormous blessings. However, the ultimate purpose of meditating on the

Scriptures is so that you can do what the Word says and walk in obedience.

Jesus said that whoever hears His Word and does it is a like a wise man who built his house on a rock.

"Therefore everyone who hears these words of Mine and puts them into practice is like a wise man who built his house on the rock."
Matthew 7:24

So it is not enough to read, or hear the Word, it must be translated into action. If you are a believer and are having challenges with obeying the Word or walking in the Word, perhaps it is because you are not meditating on the Word of God the way you should. Once you let the Word permeate your life, it will become a part of your being and will reflect in your Christian walk. Until you are living and breathing the Word, you won't be able to fulfill the requirements of a life obedient to the Word. You must meditate on the Word enough to let it take root in your heart so that it can bear the right fruit.

5. For then you will make your way prosperous and have good success.

Wow! Who wouldn't want to be guaranteed success? If you do these things, only good fortune will come to you.

"Blessed is the one who does not walk in step with the wicked or stand in the way that sinners take or sit in the company of mockers, but whose delight is in the law of the Lord, and who meditates on His law day and night. That person is like a tree planted by streams of water, which yields its fruit in season and whose leaf does not wither—whatever they do prospers." Psalm 1:1-3

This verse describes success that will not be in just one area but in all areas of your life. Relationships will be successful, you will have a successful job, and everywhere you go and all the things that you do will be successful. In very challenging times you will not crumble; you will have the strength to go on.

I truly believe that my life mission is to help change lives. I think God has chosen this path for me, and when He calls on me to use my talent, I listen.

I had been mentoring a very special young man for a while. I was helping him become stronger in his Christian faith. One day, I asked him and a group of young people if they would meditate on the Word and reflect on how it affected them. I wanted to show them what happens when you start memorizing the scriptures. It is important to realize that sometimes, you can believe things in your head but not necessarily in your heart. How do you get it into your heart, where you actually believe it and live it? You meditate. How often? Day and night.

This young man and the group took my challenge and began to memorize one verse per day. After almost getting through an entire chapter, this particular person I was mentoring decided to go to a party. He felt that he could handle and resist any temptation at this event. He told me that once he was at the party, he picked up an alcoholic drink, and the verses he had memorized starting coming to his mind. He could not believe it! He immediately knew that God was speaking to his heart, and he left the party. When you get the Word inside of you, it becomes part of your being. God was telling him that He knew him from the time he was in his mother's womb. God was reminding him that He had good plans for him. The young man knew that he shouldn't be at that party, and that realization made him leave.

I tell this story over and over just to prove a point. The Word is alive! The Bible is not just a book full of stories, poems, allegories or parables. No! It is a living book that has the power to change your life. I understood this at a very young age. I could see where diving into God's Word would set me up for success. I didn't have any friends at the time, and so, it was just me and God. I jumped in and let God lead my life.

God speaks through the Bible to us. There are nuggets of hope, joy, vision and purpose that are all waiting to come your way. You can be depressed and without joy in your life, and the Word will refresh you. You might have lost your job or even your purpose in life, but the Word will energize you as it reveals your purpose to you, even in the mist of sorrow and difficulty. I have seen God move mountains in my life. There was no humanly possible way we could come out of poverty and be so successful, to the point of owning two universities, but God was able to do it. Circumstances change when the Word is working in your life. A wonderful adventure begins when you let the Word rule your life.

Sometimes, we set aside a time for devotions with God, but we are not able to focus and follow through. We get distracted by all of our worries and concerns. Moreover, these days, as our dependence on technology increases, it has become increasingly hard to disconnect from our mobile devices and pay attention to spiritual things. Even while attending church, a little more focus will yield a lot.

Do you have a personal quiet time or devotional where you spend time reading the

Scriptures and meditating on the Word? And if you do, are you able to focus, or do you allow your mind to wander? Are you able to focus on the message when you are in church? It is important to think these questions through and make the right choices to ensure you get the most benefit from your time with God.

CHAPTER 3
HOW TO MEDITATE ON THE WORD

"Keep this Book of the Law always on your lips; meditate on it day and night, so that you may be careful to do everything written in it. Then you will be prosperous and successful." Joshua 1:8

We have already discussed the importance of meditating on the Word on a daily basis. The question is, how do you get into the Word day and night? We have to sleep, and we have to work or do other things besides pray all the time.

Joshua was a great leader, but he was also a family man. He had various responsibilities, much like you and I do, so obviously he was not sitting around all day reading his Bible or meditating on a scripture, and that was not all God expected him to do either.

1. Make Time

The key to being able to do all the things that need done on a daily basis and still meditate effectively is having a reverence for the Word of God and making time for it. So Joshua, as busy as he was, would still have to free up some time to spend meditating on the Word. His life and legacy depended on it, and so does ours. No matter how busy we are, we have to find a way to make time for the Word, at least on a daily basis. You can include meditating on the Word on your break or lunchtime. Your drive to and from work can also be very refreshing and rewarding if you add scriptural meditation to the mix.

2. Use Your Free Time

We all have free time. The amount may vary from person to person and in different seasons, but we all have it. Even the busiest of us do—what matters is how we use our free time. When you are not at work or otherwise engaged, do you use your free time to reflect on God and meditate on His Word?

3. Use The Sabbath

On a weekly basis, take time to have a day dedicated, not just to worshiping or serving God, but also to reflecting on the Bible's core message. Pay attention to the teaching of the Word at church or Sunday school. No matter how often the same verses are used or who is ministering, you should never come to a place where you think, I know that scripture by heart; I don't need to hear it again or think about it. No, there is always something to be learned and received from the Word of God, no matter how often we have heard it.

4. All The Time

Sometimes we find ourselves in seasons where we are constantly on the go. This is where the discipline and investment we made in the slower seasons begin to pay off. We can meditate on the go. The Word should always be at the back of your mind and should be the foundation of all your thoughts and actions.

5. Make It A Daily and Early Routine

Marilyn Hickey is a mentor of mine, and she taught me to say my confessions in the morning while drinking my coffee. She told me to always be ready to confess the Word. For my daily time with God, I love to put my daily confession scriptures in a special notebook I use just for that purpose. I keep that notebook with me all the time so that if I have spare time I can pull it out and meditate. I constantly find new scriptures and add them to my daily confessions.

Every morning, I wake up to a set of scriptures that I am ready to meditate on. I say them out loud so I can hear them, or if I am at a coffee shop, I just read them quietly. This is part of my daily devotion time. Sometimes, I run out of time in the morning, and I catch up with them on the run. Perhaps during lunch, or at another point in my day, I will try to find time to meditate. I make sure to take time to say them every day. I have been doing this for over 25 years now, and I can guarantee you that the success I have experienced in every area of my life is directly related to taking time to get the Word into my spirit.

I want you to start taking time to go through the Scriptures each day. Find verses that you need for certain situations, and begin reading them aloud daily. Find the verses that will bring you peace and understanding during trying times.

Let me share with you another story. I was helping at a youth camp, and the camp leaders challenged the youth to memorize scriptures. It was brilliant. These young people ranged in age from 6th grade through college. The goal was to memorize the most scriptures and to say them out loud to the leader of your team. At the end of the week, whoever had the most scriptures memorized would be the winner.

I just laughed under my breath, and thought that this would be interesting to watch. Remember that the Word is alive, and when you begin to memorize it, things happen. The Word will do what it says it will do. You just have to make the effort to get it from the Bible into your head and from the mind into your heart.

I predicted that these young people would start to change and act differently. I was waiting for hearts to change right in front of me. And truly, as the camp meetings continued and they heard different speakers, many of the young people would break down and allow the Holy Spirit to work in their lives. There were more smiles and even anticipation of God's purpose for life. The Word of God had made a difference in their lives in just one short week.

When you memorize or meditate on the Word, you become more open to hear what God is trying to say to you. Everything starts becoming clearer regarding your future and God's purposes for your life. Every day, we have to fight against the heaviness of the world that weighs us down. If we aren't careful, things will start to bother us about life, family and our future. Our secret weapon against these things is the Word. As it gets inside of us, it gives us peace and reassures us that everything in our lives will work out. Memorizing the Word will change your life! Try doing it with your family and see what happens.

Most of us have someone we are praying for that needs to be saved or perhaps healed of sickness. In these situations, we need a scripture to stand on and attach our faith to. Maybe your confidence is not where it should be for an upcoming job interview. A scripture about God's help, His favor or His good plans for you will give the courage you lack.

How about praying over your young children? Or praying for God to bring you a spouse (if you are unmarried)? God wants to get into every area of your life and give you hope and comfort. How does He do that? Many times, it is through His Word and your confessions.

REASONS TO CONFESS THE WORD

1. When you confess the Word, it gives you hope that nothing else can.

I can be hopeless and in a bad mood, but my time in the Word is what brings me back into a good mindset before I start my day. You have to realize that before you get to work (or school) each day, you will run into all kinds of people who may need your positive spirit to encourage them. You need to be ready for divine appointments that might come your way. Remember that you could be the only example of Jesus those people ever encounter. Be ready!

2. You will begin to fine-tune your spiritual ears so you can hear what God is directing you to do.

It probably won't be audible (although don't you wish it was?), but if you know how to listen, God speaks through the Scriptures. He gives you new ideas for work, new structures, systems and strategies for your ministry, and keeps you calm during the storms of life.

3. Peace will be with you.

Things won't bother you as much. You will

walk in peace more than ever before. Reading the Word and confessing it brings healing to situations in your life. Remember that the Word works for you.

4. Our character changes, and God uses circumstances to get us closer to Him.

We become more Christlike in how we deal with people. We begin to stop judging and start seeing people through the eyes of Jesus. Our ability to relate to people with love and respect is key to our success in life, and as we meditate on the Word, we bear the fruit of the Spirit that enables us to successfully relate to and manage people well. We begin to have the fruit of the Spirit—love, joy, peace, forbearance, kindness, goodness, faithfulness, gentleness and self-control—shining through us. The Word cleanses us and makes us better people, managers, co-workers, friends, etc., which leads to success in the workplace. After all, who wouldn't want to recommend a good friend, boss or subordinate?

5. Confessing the Scriptures will set you up for success.

Prosperity will come in every area of your life. Wherever you go, you will have uncommon favor. Things that you expect to be difficult will be unusually easy. Even if you find yourself in tough situations, the Word will make all things work out for your good, and you will always come out on top.

Have I convinced you of the importance of scriptural meditation? Now, let's get in the Word and make it a daily part of your time with God.

CHAPTER 4
MY FAVORITE DAILY CONFESSIONS

In this chapter, I give you some passages of the Bible that will help you develop the discipline of confessing the Scriptures. Some have been paraphrased to help with readability. You can either read through (and confess) all these verses in about 10 minutes, or you can pick and choose what you need depending on what you are going through at the time. I recommend confessing all these scriptures at once. It is a great way to start your day.

I read these scriptures daily. Even if you are pressed for time, be sure to read these scriptures over yourself and your family. Then, as you can, add the other confessions in the following chapters (grouped by subject).

"*Now faith is confidence in what we hope for and assurance about what we do not see.*" (Hebrews 11:1)

"*For the Word of God is living and powerful, and sharper than any two-edged sword, piercing even to the division of soul and spirit, and of joints and marrow, and is a discerner of the thoughts and intents of the heart.*" (Hebrews 4:12)

"*The wise will hear and increase their learning, and the person of understanding will acquire wise counsel and the skill [to steer his course wisely and lead others to the truth].*" (Proverbs 1:5 AMP)

"*If any of you is deficient in wisdom, let him ask of the giving God, Who gives it every day.*" (James 1:5)

"Wisdom is the principal thing; therefore get wisdom. And in all your getting, get understanding."
(Proverbs 4:7)

"Let wisdom and knowledge be my stability and the strength of my salvation, and the fear of the Lord my treasure."
(Isaiah 33:6 NKJV)

"Open my eyes that I may see wonderful things in your law." (Psalm 119:18)

"Let me have grace for understanding proverbs and parables, the sayings and riddles of the wise." (Proverbs 1:6)

"I pray that all spiritual cataracts and scales be removed from my eyes."
(Acts 9:18)

"Open my mind to understand the deep things of God!"(1 Corinthians 2:10)

"You are a God Who reveals secrets unto me." (Daniel 2:28 NKJV)

"Let the hidden things be revealed." (Mark 4:22 NKJV)

"The Kingdom of God is righteousness, peace and joy in the Holy Spirit." This is my inheritance and mine for the taking! (Romans 14:17)

"'For I know the plans I have for you,' declares the LORD, 'plans to prosper you and not to harm you, plans to give you hope and a future.'" (Jeremiah 29:11)

"Let the years of my life increase." (Proverbs 9:11)

"Lord, this is my set time for favor." (Psalm 102:13)

"I will make rivers flow on barren heights, and springs within the valleys.

I will turn the desert into pools of water, and the parched ground into springs."
(Isaiah 41:18)

"I pray for the floodgates of Heaven to be opened over my life."
(Malachi 3:10)

"Lord, open rivers in high places for me and fountains in the midst of my valley." (Isaiah 41:18)

"Let the heavens drop dew upon my life. "(Deuteronomy 33:28)

"A man's gift makes room for him, and brings him before great men."
(Proverbs 18:16 NKJV)

"I will obtain joy and gladness; sadness and sorrow will flee from my life."
(Isaiah 35:10)

"Lord, in every desert place in my life command Your blessing. Fill the desert with all kinds of trees, cedars, acacias and myrtles, olive and cypress trees, fir trees, and pines." (Isaiah 41:19)

"The righteous person faces many troubles, but the Lord comes to the rescue each time." (Psalm 34:19 NLT)

"I will wait upon the Lord and renew my strength." (Isaiah 40:31)

"I will not fear, for You, Lord, will hold my hand and help me." (Isaiah 41:13)

"In quietness and confidence shall be my strength." (Isaiah 30:15 NKJV)

"When Jesus had called the Twelve together, He gave them power and authority to drive out all demons and to cure diseases." (Luke 9:1)

"Behold I give unto you authority to trample on serpents and scorpions, and to overcome all the power of the enemy; and nothing will harm you."
(Luke 10:19)

"But you will receive power when the Holy Spirit comes on you…" *(Acts 1:8)*

"I desire to move in the gifts of the Holy Spirit, and I pray that the gift of prophesy will come over me and my house." *(1 Corinthians 14:1)*

"Let the arm of the Lord be revealed in my life in a mighty way." *(John 12:38)*

"I pray for angels to be released, and I stand against any spirit in the heavens assigned to block my prayers from being answered." *(Daniel 10:12-13)*

"*Therefore submit to God. Resist the devil and he will flee from you.*"
(James 4:8 NKJV)

"*I take my position in the heavens and bind the principalities and powers that operate against my life in the name of Jesus.*" (Ephesians 2:6)

"*I break and rebuke every program in the heavens that would operate against me through the sun, moon, the stars and the constellations.*"
(Psalm 121:5-6; Judges 5:20)

"*I pursued my enemies and overtook them; I did not turn back till they were destroyed.*" (Psalm 18:37)

"*May all my enemies be disgraced and terrified; may they suddenly turn back in shame.*" (Psalm 6:10)

"I will not fear though tens of thousands assail me on every side." (Psalm 3:6)

"I will not die but live, and will proclaim what the LORD has done." (Psalm 118:17)

"You will keep me in perfect peace because my mind is stayed on You, and I trust in You." (Isaiah 26:3 NKJV)

"Let me live in a peaceful dwelling place, and in secure homes, in undisturbed places of rest." (Isaiah 32:18)

"I hear the voice of the Lord; He tells me the way. When I should turn to the right or the left, He counsels me to walk in His way."(Isaiah 30:21)

"...The soul of the diligent shall be made rich." (Proverbs 13:4)

"*But my delight is in the law of the Lord, and in His law I meditate day and night. I shall be like a tree planted by the rivers of water, that brings forth its fruit in its season, whose leaf also shall not wither; and whatever I do shall prosper.*" *(Psalm 1:2-3 NKJV)*

CHAPTER 5
SCRIPTURE-INSPIRED CONFESSIONS

An important principle of success is positive thinking. No one who has a negative outlook on life can achieve anything of importance. However, while having positive thought processes is helpful for success, it is also important to reflect that positivity in the words you say and how you say them. For instance, it is better to say, "The glass is half full," than to declare it half empty. Positive words can inspire confidence, bring comfort and promote personal perseverance.

In spite of how powerful and useful positive thinking and confessions are, they can only take you so far because they don't have the power of the Hoiy Spirit. Jesus said:

"The Spirit gives life; the flesh counts for nothing. The words I have spoken to you—they are full of the Spirit and life." John 6:63

Only the Holy Scriptures have the creative and life-giving power of the Holy Spirit. The

Word can also inspire, comfort and strengthen your determination, but it does even more than that. The Word is full of life, and it nourishes both the spirit and the soul, bringing healing to the body.

In this chapter I share with you some powerful confessions. These are not just positive words or great sayings. They are inspired by and based on the Scriptures. It is a good habit to paraphrase verses and speak them over your life or apply them to a given situation. I hope these confessions will spark your desire and commitment to confessing the Word over your life and the lives of your loved ones.

CONFESSIONS ON
THE WORD & WISDOM

THE POWER OF YOUR WORD

"In Your unfailing love preserve my life, that I may obey the statutes of Your mouth. Your word, Lord, is eternal; it stands firm in the heavens. Your faithfulness continues through all generations; You established the Earth, and it endures." *Psalm 119:88-90*

O*h Lord, Your word stands firm in the heavens. It cannot be changed or made void. Let it be unto me as it is written concerning me in the heavens. Let my life be precious in Your sight, and let me live to fulfill all of my days according to what You have purposed in Your heart for me. Let me experience Your unfailing love in everything I do, and let my children's children also experience Your grace and mercy in the New Covenant.*

THE WORD ACCOMPLISHES ALL

"As the rain and the snow come down from Heaven, and do not return to it without watering the Earth and making it bud and flourish, so that it yields seed for the sower and bread for the eater, so is My word that goes out from My mouth: It will not return to Me empty, but will accomplish what I desire and achieve the purpose for which I sent it." *Isaiah 55:10-11*

Creator of the heavens and the Earth, by Your word You created the entire universe and everything in it. The whole creation is sustained by Your powerful Word. There is nothing that is too difficult for You or beyond Your power to perform. Lord, I acknowledge that You have a unique assignment and purpose for my life. Let every word spoken over my life be accomplished, and let none of Your promises return to You unfulfilled.

LET THE WORD SANCTIFY ME

"Sanctify them by the truth; Your Word is truth." *John 17:17*

*F*ather God, as I dig into Your Word in prayer and meditation, I ask that the cleansing power of Your Word be activated in me. Purge my mind, my heart, my spirit, soul and body with Your Truth. Let my thinking be renewed, and bring transformation to every area of my life. By the power of Your Word, separate me unto Yourself. Separate me from the pack, bring favor to my life and distinguish me. Let Your Word work in me, and let my full destiny and purpose be unleashed. By the power of Your Word, I am sanctified for Your glory and separated to serve You and to be a success in life.

THE WISDOM OF THE WORD

"Let the wise listen and add to their learning, and let the discerning get guidance–for understanding proverbs and parables, the saying and riddles of the wise." *Proverbs 1:5-6*

Gracious Lord, give me a listening ear, so that I would pay attention to Your Word and listen to Your voice. Add to my wisdom and understanding. Give me insight into Your Word, and let me have revelation knowledge of the Bible. Increase my knowledge and understanding of Your ways as well as Your Kingdom, and help me to comprehend dreams, parables and riddles of the wise. Help me to never lack counsel when I need it. Guide me in every aspect of my life and in all of my dealings and affairs. Give me wisdom from Your Word to apply to every situation of my life.

I NEED YOUR WISDOM

"If any of you lacks wisdom, you should ask God, Who gives generously to all without finding fault, and it will be given to you."
James 1:5

Eternal Father, you are ever merciful and generous beyond measure to all of Your children. I acknowledge my lack of wisdom, and I humbly request that You give me wisdom to live this life successfully. I stand on Your promise that when I ask, You will give generously. Therefore, give me wisdom for every area of my life—my walk with You, my family, my career and my finances. Let me find knowledge and wisdom in the Scriptures. Let Your Spirit of wisdom and counsel come upon me. Like Your prophet Daniel, let there be no problem too difficult for me to solve.

I LOVE THE SCRIPTURES

"But they delight in the law of the Lord, meditating on it day and night. They are like trees planted along the riverbank, bearing fruit each season. Their leaves never wither, and they prosper in all they do." *Psalms 1:2-3 NLT*

Light of the world, Your Word is a lamp unto my feet and a light unto my path. I take great pleasure in meditating on Your Word. Let me be like a tree that is planted by a river, and let my soul always be refreshed with the presence of Your Holy Spirit. I pray that You will establish me and that my roots will go deep into the Rock which is Christ Jesus. Let me be strong and unmovable. And no matter the season I am in, let me stay strong spiritually and be fruitful. May Your blessings always abound in my life.

Confessions on Submission & Surrender

GOD IS MY FIRST PRIORITY

"But seek first His Kingdom and His righteousness, and all these things will be given to you as well." *Matthew 6:33*

Heavenly Father, I desire to please You in all that I do. I make it my first priority in life to fulfill Your will and Your purposes. Fill my heart with joy, and let me pursue peace with all men. Let me walk in Your righteousness and in the power of Your Holy Spirit. Lord, as I make Your Kingdom my utmost priority, You also make my needs Your priority. Let all my personal and material needs be met, without me even asking. Supply my every need according to Your riches in glory by Christ Jesus. Let me always have more than enough for myself and for others. Use me as a conduit to bless others.

I SURRENDER EVERYTHING

"…But as for me and my household, we will serve the Lord." *Joshua 24:15*

Lord of the heavens and the Earth, in a time when many have forsaken the paths of righteousness, I make a commitment to seek Your ways. I surrender totally and completely to You. You are the Lord over my life, over everything I own, over all the works of my hands and over my destiny. I commit myself, my family and my entire household to serving You all the days our lives. I will not sway from Your good way in times of adversity. I will stand on Your Word, and I will see the salvation of the Lord. In times of prosperity, I will testify of Your goodness and mercy toward me, that all may know that indeed to the faithful, You show Yourself faithful.

IN GOD I TRUST

"Trust in the Lord with all of your heart and lean not on your own understanding; in all your ways submit to Him and He will make your paths straight." *Proverbs 3:5-6*

Almighty God, let me not be a victim of my own pride or haughtiness. Help me to realize that I do not know everything. You are Almighty, and I trust You with every aspect of my life. You are omnipotent, omniscient and omnipresent. You see all, You hear all and You know all—the past, the present and the future. Therefore, I will trust You with all my decisions, whether in my personal life or career, knowing that I will never go wrong if You guide me.

Lord, bring purpose and direction to my life and make my paths straight.

CHANGE MY DESIRES TO YOURS

"Take delight in the Lord, and He will give you the desires of your heart." *Psalm 37:4*

Great Redeemer, I take pleasure in You and in all of Your interests in the Earth. I surrender wholly and totally to You from this day forward, and I commit to engage in Your redemptive work. I do not hold back. Use me as an instrument of transformation and change wherever I go. Let Your kingdom come, and let Your purposes manifest in my life and in the lives of others. Let my desires be aligned with Yours, and let me see as You see, hear as You hear and touch as You do to bring healing to all. Lord, bring fulfillment to every need and desire of mine, like only You can, and let my life be pleasing to You.

I WILL NOT CONFORM

"Therefore, I urge you, brothers and sisters, in view of God's mercy, to offer your bodies as a living sacrifice, holy and pleasing to God—this is your true and proper worship. Do not conform to the pattern of this world, but be transformed by the renewing of your mind. Then you will be able to test and approve what God's will is—His good, pleasing and perfect will." *Romans 12:1-2*

Heavenly Father, I thank You for Your mercies that are new every morning. I make it a priority to please You in all that I do. I surrender my will and my ambitions, and I offer my body as a living sacrifice to You and to Your purposes. I will not conform to the systems, patterns and expectations of this world, but will surrender only to Your will and to Your expectations and requirements of me. By the power of Your Word, let my mind be renewed.

Give me the mind of Christ, and let me be transformed into the person You have called me to be. Let Your kingdom manifest in my life, and let me prove Your good, perfect and acceptable will.

CONFESSIONS ON
FAITH & HOPE

I COME IN FAITH

"And without faith it is impossible to please God, because anyone who comes to Him must believe that He exists and that He rewards those who earnestly seek Him." *Hebrews 11:6*

Father God, I thank You for faith that pleases You. I believe that You created the world and all that is within it. You are a God of mercy who rewards those who diligently seek You. Renew my zeal and grant me grace to seek You earnestly from this day forward. Lord, I am not serving you for the reward, but be merciful unto me and remember me. Let me not toil and struggle in life. Pour out Your blessings upon me, and let me experience success in every area of my life. Every day of my life, I will testify of Your goodness toward those who seek You.

I LIVE BY FAITH IN THE WORD

"For we live by faith, not by sight."
2 Corinthians 5:7

*E*ver faithful Lord, I live by faith and not by sight. I choose to believe in Your Word and Your amazing promises for my life. I acknowledge that there are things that are real, but cannot be seen, and I believe that there are things You are doing on my behalf that I don't know or understand. I do not lean on my own understanding but rather on the Word of God. I will not be moved by my present circumstances but only by the Word of God. I see myself overcoming every situation in my life, family and career. I see new doors opening for me and a total restoration of things that I *have lost. I believe that You have a great future in store for me, and I will see it come to pass in my life.*

I ASK AND I RECEIVE

"Therefore, I tell you, whatever you ask for in prayer, believe that you have received it, and it will be yours." *Mark 11:24*

Father God, I depend on Your Word. Your promises are yea and Amen in Christ Jesus. I take Your Word at face value, and I believe whatever the Scriptures say. You know my needs to every last detail and all the things that I am praying for in my life, family, career and destiny. I am confident that You hear my prayers, and I believe that I have received the answers that I seek. You are able to exceed my expectations. I wait in faith and patience for what You have promised. I will not let my circumstances discourage me. Thank

You for always hearing my prayers; You are fully trustworthy.

(I WILL WAIT IN HOPE)

"Against all hope, Abraham in hope believed and so became the father of many nations, just as it had been said to him, 'So shall your offspring be.' Without weakening in his faith, he faced the fact that his body was as good as dead—since he was about a hundred years old—and that Sarah's womb was also dead. Yet he did not waver through unbelief regarding the promise of God, but was strengthened in his faith and gave glory to God."
Romans 4:18-20

My Father in Heaven, my hope is in You regarding Your promises for my life. In spite of what the circumstances seem to be, or any appearance of delay, I will not be weakened in my faith. I will continue to put my hope in Your unfailing love. I believe in Your power to perform that which You have promised me, and I believe that in due season You will bring me to my expected end. Let Your resurrection power come upon me and bring to life every dead hope and dream. Let there be increase and multiplication in my life that I may testify of Your faithfulness to all.

I WILL WAIT IN PATIENCE

"We do not want you to become lazy, but to imitate those who through faith and patience inherit what has been promised."
Hebrews 6:12

G od of Abraham, Isaac and Jacob, I thank You for the testimonies of those who have gone before me in the faith, and the cloud of witnesses that surrounds me. Grant me the grace to pay attention to words of encouragement in the Scriptures, and above all, let me be a doer of the Word and not just a hearer. I pray for the spirit of diligence in my walk with You. Wake me up from every spiritual slumber. Lord, deliver me from every tendency to be hasty in my decisions and choices, and give me the grace to be patient in faith and hope as I wait for the manifestation of Your promises in my life.

I WILL SOAR LIKE THE EAGLE

"But those who hope in the Lord will renew their strength. They will soar on wings like eagles; they will run and not grow weary, they will walk and not be faint." *Isaiah 40:31*

*S*overeign Lord, I put my hope in You. You are the source of all my hope and strength. Give me the courage to wait upon You no matter how stressed or hard pressed I am. Infuse me with strength, and let my youth be renewed like the eagles. Touch my body and soul with Your life-giving power, and let me be rejuvenated. Because I hope in You, I *will not be put to shame. I will run and not grow weary, I will walk and not be faint. I have the strength of a wild ox, and I have the grace and power to go the extra mile and to overcome every difficulty.*

Confessions
on Love

$$\boxed{\text{UNCONDITIONAL LOVE}}$$

"For God so loved the world that He gave His one and only Son, that whoever believes in Him shall not perish but have eternal life." *John 3:16*

Father God, Your love is so true and so thorough that it is beyond comprehension. Your love for me is unconditional. It has never changed, and it is ever strong. You so love the world and everyone in it that You allowed Your only Son Jesus to die and redeem the Earth from judgment. Father, I believe in Your Son Jesus Christ. I believe that on the cross He paid a penalty for my sin that I might have life and have it eternally and abundantly. I believe that on the third day, by the power of Your

Holy Spirit, He rose again from the dead, and He has ascended to sit at Your right hand. Now, that same Holy Spirit is at work in me. I pray that I will experience Your resurrection power in every area of my life. Let all the chains of sickness, death and of destruction be broken off of me, and let me take my place in Your Kingdom.

I HAVE THE CAPACITY TO LOVE

"Jesus replied: 'Love the Lord your God with all your heart and with all your soul and with all your mind. This is the first and greatest commandment. And the second is like it: Love your neighbor as yourself.'" *Matthew 22:37-39*

G od of Love, I thank You that You created me in Your own image and likeness. I am an emotional being with the capacity to love God and to love my fellow human beings. Help me to express my love to You freely in worship. Let me not hold back in my walk with You. Help me to put value on myself and to see myself as You do so that I may love myself, my life and all its intricacies. Let me appreciate my uniqueness and talents as a person, my calling and destiny, as well as all that You have in store for me. Give me the grace to love my family and serve all the people in my life sacrificially. Touch my heart, and let me love others as much as I love myself with the amazing love that You have shown me.

MY LOVE IS FORGIVING

"Above all, love each other deeply, because love covers over a multitude of sins. Offer hospitality to one another without grumbling. Each of you should use whatever gift you have received to serve others, as faithful stewards of God's grace in its various forms."
1 Peter 4:8-10

Heavenly Father, I freely receive of the Love that sent Your Son Jesus Christ to die on the cross. Your Agape love is powerful enough to cover all my sins, iniquities and transgressions. As I receive of Your love, help me to give it freely to others. Help me to love others deeply, and help me to make a deliberate, conscious and serious effort to forgive all those who have wronged me in any way. Grant me the grace not to be judgmental of those who are less fortunate or who fall short morally or in their spiritual life. Let me be a faithful steward of all the gifts and goods You have so generously bestowed on me. I make myself wholeheartedly available to serve Your people without reservation and without complaining.

MY LOVE TRANSCENDS ALL

"Love is patient, love is kind. It does not envy, it does not boast, it is not proud. It does not dishonor others, it is not self-seeking, it is not easily angered, it keeps no record of wrongs. Love does not delight in evil but rejoices with the truth. It always protects, always trusts, always hopes, always perseveres."
1 Corinthians 13:4-7

O h that my love would be a true reflection of Your grace and mercy toward me and that it would be truly divine. Lord, help me to be patient with my family, friends, colleagues and all those in my life. Help me to be kind to them when they need me. When others are prospering, let me celebrate with them and not envy them. And when my season comes and You lift me up, help me not to gloat. Help me to value people, and let me honor those You place in my care. Let me keep my emotions in check and not yield to anger when offended. When I am wronged, help me not to keep count, but let me be forgiving. When I see people suffering or experiencing injustice of any kind, may my heart be moved with compassion and my hand reach out in protection of them. May I always be hopeful that people will change, and let me not give up on people.

I AM LOVED EVEN IN MY SINS

"But God demonstrates His own love for us in this: While we were still sinners, Christ died for us." *Romans 5:8*

*M*erciful Lord, Your love for me is beyond question. While I was still a sinner, You died for me. The price for every sin I have ever committed and will ever commit has been paid in full. Help me to understand this precious and priceless love and to realize that I can never work hard enough to pay for

Your love. Indeed, there is nothing I can do to earn Your grace and forgiveness. I already have it even before I need it. Above all, help me to not despise Your sacrifice for me. Rather, let me take full advantage of it and live a fulfilled life that will impact Your Kingdom, bring hope to the world and give You glory.

Confessions on
Peace & Tranquility

MY MIND IS FIXED ON GOD

"You will keep in perfect peace those whose minds are steadfast, because they trust in You."
Isaiah 26:3

God of peace, I refuse to be disturbed even in a season of turbulence and chaos. I receive Your perfect peace that surpasses all understanding, even in this time of my life. I will not be swayed or be double-minded. My mind will continue to stay on You, on Your power, Your love and Your mercy toward me. Lord, no matter what is going on around me, I choose to trust You, being assured that You will bring me through everything in grand style. Grant me the grace to be focused on You even in the midst of the storms. Let not my heart be troubled.

Help me to be of good cheer, knowing that You have overcome the world.

I RECEIVE YOUR PEACE

"Peace I leave with you; My peace I give you. I do not give to you as the world gives. Do not let your hearts be troubled and do not be afraid." *John 14:27*

Oh Great Deliverer, I will not let my heart be troubled. I will not let my circumstances and the things I am going through weigh me down. I will not use worldly goods and carnal desires to mask my feelings and frustrations, and I will not indulge in sinful pursuits in order to drown my sorrows and the pain in my heart. You alone are the Prince of Peace and the source of my tranquility. I embrace the peace that You surround me with, and I thank You that You give me the kind of peace that the world cannot give.

PEACE GUARDS MY HEART

"And the peace of God, which transcends all understanding, will guard your hearts and your minds in Jesus Christ." *Philippians 4:7*

O *mniscient God, You know all that is going on in my life, my family and career. You are aware of all my concerns and worries about my future. In the midst of the storm, I ask for Your peace that is beyond human understanding. I repent of any tendency to be anxious. Let me not yield to the stresses of life, and deliver me from distractions. Let Your perfect peace guard my heart and my mind, and let it keep me focused on the Lord Jesus Christ. In spite of all that I am going through, I will not be swayed by the storms of life, because You reassure me.*

PEACE RULES IN MY LIFE

"Let the peace of Christ rule in your hearts, since as members of one body you were called to peace. And be thankful." *Colossians 3:15*

*D*ear Lord, I thank You that You are the Prince of Peace. You are not the author of confusion or chaos. I ask that You give me peace in every area of my life. Let Your peace have dominion over my mind, my heart, my spirit, my soul and my entire life. No matter what I am going through, or where I find myself, I will not yield to sorrow or depression. I will not let the stress of life burden me. I embrace Your peace that surpasses all understanding. I speak the peace of God into every situation in my home, my work and every area of my life. Let there be peace!

CONFESSIONS ON DELIVERANCE AND DIVINE PROTECTION

THE LORD DELIVERS ME

"The Lord will vindicate me; Your love, Lord, endures forever—do not abandon the works of Your hands." *Psalm 138:8*

Faithful Lord, I claim this promise over my life. You have promised to vindicate Your children who cry unto You day and night. Lord, I ask that You remember me, all my struggles and everything that I am going through. Look upon the shed blood of Your Son, and come to my rescue. Do not abandon me to the desires of my foes. Deliver me from the power of sickness, poverty and failure, and let all people know that indeed You love and favor me. Let my life and story be a testimony of Your goodness and mercy and not of judgment and failure. Thank You for the exceedingly great favor that You release upon me.

I AM SECURE IN GOD

"No harm will overtake you, no disaster will come near your tent. For He will command His angels concerning you to guard you in all your ways." *Psalm 91:10-11*

Heavenly Father, I am grateful for the angels You have assigned to watch over me, my family and my entire household. I thank You for the hedge of protection that is all around me on every side. All of my interests and affairs are in Your care. You surround me with favor like an impenetrable shield. No harm of any kind, shape or form comes near me. In all of my ways, whether I am at home, at work or traveling, I am guaranteed Your excellent protection. I thank You that You are always there to protect me.

GOD MAKES MY STEPS FIRM

"The Lord makes firm the steps of the one who delights in Him; though he may stumble, he will not fall, for the Lord upholds him with His hand." *Psalm 37:23-24*

Your Word is a lamp unto my feet and a light unto my path. Because I take delight in You, You make my steps firm. I am not double-minded or confused. I have clarity of thought and direction. I will not stumble in my decision-making. I am honest and dependable, but even if I stumble, I will not be caught in any traps of the enemy. I cannot and will not fall, because Your right hand holds me up. Your mighty hand keeps me from shame and reproach. I am anointed for success, and a spirit of excellence is upon me. I will prosper in all that I put my hands to, because the power of Your Spirit is at work in me.

I CAN COUNT ON GOD'S HELP

"For I am the Lord your God Who takes hold of your right hand and says to you, 'Do not fear; I will help you.'" *Isaiah 41:13*

*E*ternal Lord, I lift up my hands in worship and adoration. You are my Lord and my God, and I surrender totally to You. I thank You that You take hold of my right hand to reassure and lead me where I should go. No matter the circumstances I find myself in or the darkness that surrounds me, I will not be afraid. I will not fear the storms of life that come my way and the things that threaten my health, career and future. I thank You that I receive Your help in every area of my life and for every situation. You are with me, so I know that it is well with my soul, and I can count on Your help.

GOD'S FAVOR IS MY SHIELD

"Surely, LORD, You bless the righteous; You surround them with Your favor as with a shield." *Psalm 5:12*

Gracious Father, I am Your child, born of the Word and the Spirit and justified by faith in Christ Jesus. Pour out Your blessings beyond measure on me, and let every area of my life experience abundance and fruitfulness. Like Joseph, let a spirit of excellence come upon me and affect every area of my life. Surround me and shield me with Your favor and love; wherever I go and in whatever I do, let Your favor manifest in my life. Let me experience preferential treatment because of Your blessings and unmerited favor upon my life. Where others fail, let me succeed beyond my own expectations.

CONFESSIONS ON PRAYER & SPIRITUAL WARFARE

MY ARMOR IS DIVINE

"A final word: Be strong in the Lord and in His mighty power. Put on all of God's armor so that you will be able to stand firm against all strategies of the devil. For we are not fighting against flesh-and-blood enemies, but against evil rulers and authorities of the unseen world, against mighty powers in this dark world, and against evil spirits in the heavenly places.

Therefore, put on every piece of God's armor so you will be able to resist the enemy in the time of evil. Then after the battle you will still be standing firm. Stand your ground, putting on the belt of truth and the body armor of God's righteousness. For shoes, put on the peace that comes from the Good News so that you will be fully prepared. In addition to all of these, hold up the shield of faith to stop the fiery arrows of the devil. Put on salvation as your helmet, and take the Sword of the Spirit, which is the Word of God." *Ephesians 6:10-17 NLT*

The Lord is strong and mighty in battle. I am strong in the Lord and in His mighty power. I put on the full armor of God to wage war against the forces of darkness. I come not in my own name or power but in the name of the Lord and in the power of the Holy Spirit. I am able to stand against all the strategies and attacks of the devil in whatever form they come. I put on the the belt of truth and the body armor of God's righteousness. For shoes, I put on the peace that comes from the Good News. I take hold of my shield of faith, with which I stop the fiery arrows of the devil. I secure my helmet of salvation on my head, and I take up the Sword of the Spirit, which is the Word of God. I cannot be defeated, and I will not fail. I am victorious in Christ Jesus.

I HAVE AUTHORITY OVER EVIL

"I have given you authority to trample on snakes and scorpions and to overcome all power of the enemy; nothing will harm you."
Luke 10:19

Almighty God, You have given me strength, might and power. I am not weak. I am strong mentally, physically and spiritually. I have authority and power to crush and destroy all the power of the enemy. I am not a slave to sin or any form of addiction. I break free from every grip of Satan. Let every power that the enemy has over my life be broken. I am free in my mind, my heart, my spirit, soul and body. I am free indeed because Jesus sets me free. The blood of Jesus cleanses and purges me. Nothing that the enemy plans or throws at me will harm me, because I am secured in Christ Jesus.

I AM FROM ABOVE

"You, dear children, are from God and have overcome them, because the One Who is in you is greater than the one who is in the world."
1 John 4:4

I thank You Lord, that I am Your child, and I come from the Father above. I am seated in heavenly places with Christ Jesus my Lord and Savior. I am an overcomer. I have power to overcome sin, all evil and every power of darkness. He that is in me, the Holy Spirit, is far greater and more powerful than he that is in the world. I am in the world, but I am not of it; the power of the enemy has no influence over me. I cannot be drawn into the works and dominion of darkness. I overcome every assignment of the enemy against my purpose. I cannot fail; and I will not fail. I am victorious in everything I put my hands to.

I RESIST THE DEVIL

"Submit yourselves, then, to God. Resist the devil, and he will flee from you." *James 4:7*

I stand on the Word of God, and I take my place as a child of God. I submit to the lordship of Christ and the reign of the King of Kings. I am seated in heavenly places with Christ Jesus, and I have power to trample over serpents, scorpions and over all the power of the enemy. I will not yield any part of my life or destiny to the influence of the enemy. I stand my ground in faith, and I move forward in the name of Jesus, against every attack of the enemy. I am a conquerer. I resist all the attacks and temptations of the enemy. I break free from every power of the enemy, and I take my place in the will and purpose of God.

NO WEAPON PREVAILS

"'No weapon forged against you will prevail, and you will refute every tongue that accuses you. This is the heritage of the servants of the Lord and this is their vindication from Me,' declares the Lord." *Isaiah 54:17*

*Y*ou are the Lord of Hosts. I thank You that because I serve You, I inherit a special blessing of protection. Whether they are spiritual or otherwise, no weapon that is formed against me will prevail. I refute and disavow negative and evil words that have been spoken against me. You have neutralized every curse and made the voice of the accuser silent. The enemy has no power over my life, my destiny or anything that concerns me. My world is shaped and determined by the Word of God, and there is no limitation over my life.

Confessions on
Healing and Miracles

GOD IS MY HEALER

"He said, 'If you listen carefully to the Lord your God and do what is right in His eyes, if you pay attention to His commands and keep all His decrees, I will not bring on you any of the diseases I brought on the Egyptians, for I am the Lord, Who heals you.'" *Exodus 15:26*

Jehovah Rapha, You are the Lord my healer. I am a child of Your Kingdom, and I come to You because of the finished work of Christ, Whose obedience was complete. I come to You, not in my own righteousness but in the righteousness of Christ. You are the Lord Who heals all, and I am Your child. Heal my body, touch my soul and give me a sound mind. Let Your healing power run through me, and let me be healed of every infirmity in my body. Make me whole from the crown of my head to the soles of my feet.

THE WORD OF GOD HEALS ME

"He sent out His Word and healed them, snatching them from the door of death."

Psalm 107:20 NLT

*E*verlasting Father, Your Word is powerful and mighty to save. The whole world was created and is sustained by Your mighty Word. Lord, speak into my health and deliver me from every spirit of infirmity. Send forth Your precious, powerful, healing Word to heal me today. From the crown of my head to the soles of my feet, let the Word permeate my entire being. May I experience the healing power of Christ the Word in every area of my life and in every system and organ of my body.

Let the Word of life make me whole, and let it break me free from every power of sickness, death and destruction.

I AM WHOLE IN JESUS NAME

"Surely He took up our pain and bore our suffering, yet we considered Him punished by God, stricken by Him, and afflicted. But He was pierced for our transgressions, He was crushed for our iniquities; the punishment that brought us peace was on Him, and by His wounds we are healed." *Isaiah 53:4-5*

Healing Jesus, I thank You for the pain You bore in Your body for my healing and for the blood You shed for my deliverance and peace. Your love and sacrifice for me will not be in vain. Today, I claim my total and complete healing in my mind, my heart, my spirit, my soul and my body. I am healed in every organ and system of my body. Every cell and tissue in my body functions as You designed and purposed them to. There's nothing broken or missing in my body. I receive total restoration for my soul and peace of mind. I am whole in the name of Jesus.

LET ME ENJOY GOOD HEALTH

"Beloved, I pray that you may prosper in all things and be in health, just as your soul prospers." *3 John 1:2 NKJV*

L iving God, You created me in Your image and after Your likeness. I thank You that You have as much interest in my body as You do my soul. Lord, I pray that You would grant me the grace to continue to work out my salvation with fear and trembling, that I may live a victorious Christian life. I pray that even as my soul propers and I grow spiritually, let me continue to enjoy good health. Give me a sound mind, and by the power of Your Spirit heal my body of any obvious and hidden diseases. Let my body be strengthened that I may serve You all of my days in good health.

I FLOW IN THE SUPERNATURAL

"And these signs will accompany those who believe; in My name they will drive out demons; they will speak in new tongues; they will pick up snakes with their hands; and when they drink deadly poison, it will not hurt them at all; they will place their hands on sick people, and they will get well." *Mark 16:17-18*

G od of Miracles and Mighty Deeds, I thank You for faith to believe in divine intervention. Let Your supernatural power be active in my life, and wherever I go let Your presence be made manifest. Let it impact my prayers and my confessions. Give me divine protection, and when I pray over people, let there be tangible results and solutions; let there be healings, deliverances and breakthroughs in the lives of people. Where there is darkness, let there be Light.

CONFESSIONS ON
CHRISTIAN LIVING

IN OBEDIENCE I AM BLESSED

"All these blessings will come on you and accompany you if you obey the Lord your God." *Deuteronomy 28:2*

*F*ather God, I repent of any acts of disobedience. Give me grace to live and walk in obedience to Your commandments. Let every power of stubbornness over my life be broken. I break free from every spirit of disobedience and every tendency towards waywardness. I receive a heart of obedience. By grace, I claim Your promises. Let all the blessings You have for Your children come upon me and my household in full. I will be blessed in my laying down and in my rising up. I will be blessed in my going out and *coming in. Everything that concerns me is blessed.*

I RUN FROM SIN

"…let us throw off everything that hinders and the sin that so easily entangles. And let us run with perseverance the race marked out for us."
Hebrews 12:1

Holy Father, I come to you with a contrite heart. I repent of every habitual sin, transgression and disobedience. I break free from every bad habit and addiction and from every vicious cycle. I cast off everything that weighs me down spiritually and morally. I will not bow to peer pressure, and I will not yield my mind to bad and unholy thoughts. I will run the race that is before me with perseverance, looking unto Jesus. I have the capacitiy and the ability to pursue my dreams. I will not relent in the pursuit of God. I have the grace to be disciplined and finish my course.

I HAVE AN APETITE FOR LIFE

"For the Kingdom of God is not a matter of eating and drinking, but of righteousness, peace and joy in the Holy Spirit." *Romans 14:17*

I am born of the Word and of the Spirit. I am a child of the Kingdom of God. I have a healthy and balanced appetite for both the things of the Spirit and the natural. I am free from gluttony, debauchery, greed and the lust of the flesh. I walk in the righteousness of Christ and have the peace of God that surpasses all understanding. I have the tremendous joy of the Holy Spirit, which gives me strength. I do not yield to the pride of life, and I do not pursue the things of the world; they rather follow

*and overtake me, because I have made
the Kingdom of God my first priority.*

CHRIST IS REVEALED IN ME

"I pray that out of His glorious riches He may
strengthen you with power through His Spirit
in your inner being, so that Christ may dwell
in your hearts through faith. And I pray that
you, being rooted and established in love, may
have power, together with all the Lord's holy
people, to grasp how wide and long and high
and deep is the love of Christ."
Ephesians 3:16-18

*S*overeign Lord, out of Your glorious
and limitless riches bring hope and
revitalization to my life. Let your Holy
Spirit strengthen my spirit man, my
soul and my entire being. Let my love
for Your word increase, and let my faith
grow. Touch my character, and let my
lifestyle be Christlike. Make me stable
in every area of my life that I may bear

fruit in abundance. Uproot bitterness, hatred and jealousy from my heart, and let me be rooted and established in your Agape love.

I AM FREE FROM SHAME

"For I am not ashamed of the gospel, because it is the power of God that brings salvation to everyone who believes: first to the Jew, then to the Gentile." *Romans 1:16*

I am not ashamed to be called a Christian or a child of God. I am not ashamed of the people of God, and I am not ashamed to be associated with the Body of Christ. I am not ashamed of the gospel, for it is the power God uses to save people, regardless of their ethnicity or status in life. The Gospel has power to change lives and heal hearts. I will share my faith. I will preach and teach the Gospel. I break free from every power of shame. Shame has no power or control over my life. I will be as bold as a lion about my faith, my abilities and all that God has entrusted to me. The power of the Gospel will manifest in my life. I will bear the fruit of love, joy, peace, good health and prosperity in every area of my life.

I SPEAK WORDS THAT BUILD

"Do not let any unwholesome talk come out of your mouths, but only what is helpful for building others up according to their needs, that it may benefit those who listen."
Ephesians 4:29

Holy are You Lord. I thank You that I have power and control over my thoughts and my tongue. My thoughts are pure and pleasing to You, and every Word that comes out of my mouth is constructive, not destructive. My words bring instruction and hope. I will not use my tongue to tear myself or others down. I speak life into every area of my life. I declare blessings and success in every area of my life. I am favored wherever I go. I am not a candidate for failure. Christ is in me, and there is hope for glory. I have an amazing life and a bright future.

I AM MORE THAN A CONQUEROR

"Who shall separate us from the love of Christ? Shall trouble or hardship or persecution or famine or nakedness or danger or sword? As it is written: 'For Your sake we face death all day long; we are considered as sheep to be slaughtered.' No, in all these things we are more than conquerors through Him who loved us. For I am convinced that neither death nor life, neither angels nor demons, neither the present nor the future, nor any powers, neither height nor depth, nor anything else in all creation, will be able to separate us from the love of God that is in Christ Jesus our Lord."
Romans 8:35-39

Oh Loving God, I thank You that I can count on Your wonderful love and amazing grace. I will not let the challenges of life or of the Christian faith cause me to doubt Your love, and commitment toward me and my destiny. Indeed, nothing can separate me from Your precious, unconditional Agape love. I am loved, and I will not doubt that. In spite of all that I am experiencing, I am an overcomer. I do more than survive; I thrive, even in the midst of darkness and desert. I am more than a conqueror through Christ Jesus Who strengthes me and empowers me with His Holy Spirit.

CONFESSIONS ON
PURPOSE AND FRUITFULNESS

(I HAVE A GREAT DESTINY)

"'For I know the plans that I have for you,' declares the Lord, 'plans to prosper you and not to harm you, plans to give you a hope and a future.'" *Jeremiah 29:11*

Good and Gracious God, I thank You that You have a plan and a purpose for my life. I refuse to live my life floating aimlessly or hopelessly. Your plan for my life is amazing and beyond anything I can imagine or dream. It is not a plan to destroy or harm me; it is a plan to prosper me, to give me life in abundance, hope and a great future. I refuse to doubt Your love for me and Your goodness toward me. I will not be a failure in life. I will be a great success and have a great testimony, because that is what You desire for me—to have life and have it more abundantly.

I AM MORE THAN CAPABLE

"I can do all things through Him Who gives me strength." *Philippians 4:13*

G *reat and mighty are You, oh Lord. I am created in Your image and likeness, and I have creative talents and abilities. Stengthen and inspire me by Your Holy Spirit. I will not limit myself or what You can do through me. Nothing will keep me from fulfilling my purpose in life. I will not be limited by my ancestry, ethnicity, environment or any other factor. You equip me with strength and power from on high and with wisdom beyond my years and experience. There is no problem I cannot solve, and no hurdle I cannot overcome. I can do all things through Christ Who strengthens me, and I can be great at anything I am involved in because of Your power and blessing upon my life.*

I AM POWERED BY YOUR SPIRIT

"'…Not by might nor by power, but by my Spirit,' says the Lord Almighty."
Zechariah 4:6

L ord Almighty, I confess that it is not by my might or power but by Your Spirit that I accomplish anything. In my own strength and wisdom, I cannot prevail. I thank You for Your strength and that You enable me by the power of the Holy Spirit. I am capable of fulfilling every role and calling. I can be a good parent, because You give me strength. Because of Your strength, I cannot fail in my career. I can be a success in business and ministry, because You give me strength. Because You strengthen me,

I am able to endure all trials, overcome every temptation and become a success in life.

I AM ANOINTED TO SERVE

"The Spirit of the Lord is on me, because He has anointed me to proclaim good news to the poor. He has sent me to proclaim freedom for the prisoners and recovery of sight for the blind, to set the oppressed free." *Luke 4:18*

Christ Jesus, I present myself to be used for Your purposes. Let Your Holy Spirit come upon me in might and power. Anoint me wherever I go. May I be a conduit of Your love and peace. Let those who are bound experience freedom and liberty because of Your power on my life. Through me, Lord, heal blind eyes, and use me to bring vision and hope to those who have no purpose. Wherever I find myself, let me be an agent of liberation to free those who are in any form of oppression or captivity.

I WORK WITH DILIGENCE

"A sluggard's appetite is never filled, but the desires of the diligent are fully satisfied."
Proverbs 13:4

Almighty God, you created work. In six days you created the heavens and the earth. I repent of every laziness in my life. Help me to break out of every tendency to be lazy or mediocre. Let a spirit of excellence come upon me; let me be diligent in everything that concerns me and all that you commit into my care. Lord, remember Your promise and satisfy my desires fully with good things. Bless the work of my hands. Let me eat of the fruit of my labors. Let me not labor in vain. Let me not sow for another to reap. As I sow, let me reap a good measure, pressed down, shaken together and overflowing. I will reap bountifully because I am able to sow bountifully in all things.

I EXPERIENCE OPEN HEAVENS

"I will make rivers flow on barren heights, and springs within the valleys. I will turn the desert into pools of water, and the parched ground into springs." *Isaiah 41:18*

Faithful Lord and Father, I claim this promise over my life. Let that which seems impossible with man become possible in my life. Let a new day dawn over me. Let there be open heavens over my life, and let every drought and famine in my life cease from this day forward. Let every barren area in my life experience fruitfulness, and let me experience refreshing in every dry area. Lord, I speak life, peace and joy into every area of my life—my family, my career and my ministry. I will thirst no more, because You send times of refreshing upon my life.

MY PORTION IS ABUNDANCE

"The thief comes only to steal and kill and destroy; I have come that they may have life, and have it to the full." *John 10:10*

L iving Jesus, in spite of my current circumstances and all that I am going through, I am assured of Your continued love. You love me and have only my best interest at heart. I am not confused about Your intentions concerning me. You have not come to deny me or take away from my life. You desire to add to my life, and You are actively working to multiply unto me. You have come that I may have life and have it more abundantly. In all things,

You desire to bless me mightily and have my cup overflow. Let Your goodness and mercy follow me all the days of my life.

I AM PLANTED BY STREAMS

"Blessed is the one who does not walk in step with the wicked or stand in the way that sinners take or sit in the company of mockers, but whose delight is in the law of the Lord, and who meditates on His law day and night. That person is like a tree planted by streams of water, which yields its fruit in season and whose leaf does not wither—whatever they do prospers." *Psalm 1:1-3*

Lord, I take delight in Your Word, and I make it a priority to meditate on it day and night. I do not live like one who does not know You, and I do not consult with those who despise Your Word. I do not find pleasure in the company of people who have strayed from Your path. Let my roots go deep, my foundations be strengthened, and let me be established in Your purpose. No matter the season or prevailing circumstances, help me to stay encouraged and hopeful with unyielding faith. At all times and in all things, I will rise to the occasion with wisdom that produces results and solutions through the power of Your Holy Spirit.

MY HANDS ARE BLESSED

"May the favor of the Lord our God rest on us; establish the work of our hands for us— yes, establish the work of our hands."
Psalm 90:17

My Lord and Creator, I know of a certainty that of my own accord and in my own strength there is nothing I can achieve. I yield to the power, wisdom and leadership of the Holy Spirit. In everything I do, let Your favor rest on me. Wherever I go, let me experience favor in increasing measure. Lord, let the works of my hands be pleasing to You. Let me be a conduit of Your grace and mercy to a hurting world. Bless my life, and may my fruit increase and grow from generation to generation.

CONFESSIONS ON GIVING, DIVINE PROVISION & GRATITUDE

MY GIFT MAKES A WAY

"A gift opens the way and ushers the giver into the presence of the great." *Proverbs 18:16*

Oh Giver of Life, give me a generous disposition and help me to be kind and compassionate to others regardless of their status in life, ethnicity or religious affiliation. As I receive from you, let me freely give to others both great and small. And let me also benefit from the generosity of others. You are the Lord my Shepherd, and I shall never be in want. Oh Sovereign Lord, order my gifts and my steps into great doors, great opportunities and divine appointments. Order my steps into the lives of great and influential people. Give me exceptional gifts and talents that will make me stand out from the crowd, and grant me a platform for my gifts and talents to bless and impact multitudes.

ALL I HAVE IS FROM YOU

"Honor the Lord with your wealth, with the first fruits of all your crops; then your barns will be filled to overflowing, and your vats will brim over with new wine." *Proverbs 3:9-10*

S overeign Lord and Creator, I acknowledge that all that I am and whatever I have is a gift from You. The success I have achieved is because of Your favor and blessing upon my life. I will honor You with my wealth and the first fruits of every blessing You give me. As You have promised, bring increase and multiplication to my life. Let there be overflow of blessing and prosperity over everything I put my hands to. Let poverty, failure and shame be utterly banished from my life. Bless me with good health, joy, peace and fulfillment.

I WILL BE FAITHFUL TO TITHE

"'Bring the whole tithe into the storehouse, that there may be food in My house. Test Me in this,' says Lord Almighty, 'and see if I will not throw open the floodgates of Heaven and pour out so much blessing that there will not be room enough to store it.'" *Malachi 3:10*

O mnipotent Father, I repent of any unfaithfulness in tithing. Renew my thinking regarding this blessed privilege to serve and fund your Kingdom. Restore to me a spirit of gratitude and generosity. Lord, as I am faithful in tithing and giving to Your purposes, prove Your Word to me, and open the floodgates of Heaven. Let me be blessed beyond measure, as You have promised, far beyond anything I could ever imagine.

Rebuke the devourer for my sake, and let Your blessings increase in every area of my life.

THE LORD PROVIDES FOR ME

"The LORD is my shepherd, I lack nothing. He makes me lie down in green pastures, He leads me beside quiet waters, He refreshes my soul. He guides me along the right paths for His name's sake." *Psalm 23:1-3*

S hepherd of my soul, I thank you that as the Good Shepherd takes care of His sheep, so You take care of me. You are patient, kind and gentle with me. Because You lead me, I have no need of anything. I can trust You to provide only the very best for me. By the power of Your Spirit, You satisfy deep spiritual thirsts in me and bring refreshing to my soul. Because You watch over me, I am protected on all sides. It does not matter where I find myself or what I am going through, I cannot and will not be intimidated. I will not yield to the temptation to be afraid. Because You are in charge of my life, I will live and walk in faith, hope and joy, knowing that it is well with every aspect of my life.

I GIVE UNTO OTHERS FREELY

"Heal the sick, raise the dead, cleanse those who have leprosy, drive out demons. Freely you have received; freely give." *Matthew 10:8*

My Lord and Redeemer, I thank You that by the power of Your Spirit, You heal me and deliver me. And Lord, as You have touched me graciously, so let Your power and love rest on me in abundance. As I have received an abundance of grace, talents and mercy, let me also give freely to others in need. May my life be poured out for others, bringing healing and deliverance wherever I go.

I GIVE AND I RECEIVE

"Give, and it will be given to you. A good measure, pressed down, shaken together and running over, will be poured into your lap. For with the measure you use, it will be measured to you." *Luke 6:38*

*G*racious and Merciful Lord, grant me the grace to be generous in my giving. Let me not hold back my kindness and love when others are in need. As I give unto others, let me also receive. Let others be generous to me. In my time of need, let me not lack help; let there be timely help. Let help come to me from the north, the south, the east and the west. Let me find favor with others. Let even people I do not know be generous to me.

I REJOICE AND GIVE THANKS

"Rejoice always, pray continually, give thanks in all circumstances; for this is God's will for you in Christ Jesus." *1 Thessalonians 5:16-18*

Heavenly Father, I may not always feel grateful in difficult circumstances, but help me to always give thanks, regardless of what I feel. As I seek Your face, praying continually, let Your joy bring me strength. I will rejoice, knowing You are in control. I choose to walk out Your will in my life. I will be thankful in all situations. I will not worry, complain, or be afraid. I will rejoice ALWAYS!

I WILL ALWAYS PRAISE HIM

"I will extol the LORD at all times; His praise will always be on my lips." *Psalm 34:1*

You are worthy to receive all praise and adoration. I extol You Lord. I celebrate You and Your wonderful deeds. I look at Your creation… how wonderful You have made us all! How excellent is Your name, oh Lord! I lift You higher than everything surrounding me. Your name is higher than every other name that exists on Earth, and I choose to look to You rather than at my circumstances. I choose words of life, trust and faith today. Your praise will ALWAYS be on my lips.

BLESS THE LORD OH MY SOUL

"Praise the LORD, my soul; all my inmost being, praise His holy name. Praise the LORD, my soul, and forget not all His benefits— Who forgives all your sins and heals all your diseases, Who redeems your life from the pit and crowns you with love and compassion, Who satisfies your desires with good things so that your youth is renewed like the eagle's." *Psalm 103:1-5*

*B*less the Lord oh my soul, and all that is within me bless His holy name. Today, I am ever grateful for Your gift of redemption. You have forgiven me, You have healed me, You have given me a new name, written in the Lamb's Book of Life. I can never repay such gifts… and yet, You are not done. You satisfy my desires with good things; You actually know, care about and fulfill my desires. You are a good Father, and as Your child, I rest in You. I praise You for what You have done, but more than that, I praise You for Who You are. Redeemer. Life-Giver. Lover of my soul. Strength-Giver. Compassionate Father. In You I trust today. My soul blesses You, for Your mercies are truly new every morning.

CHAPTER 6
PERSONALIZED CONFESSIONS

I like to personalize scriptures that really minister to me. This is a practical way to apply the scriptures to your life. When I take words from the Bible and make them my own, it helps me to actually live them.

To personalize a scripture, insert your name and/or that of your family into the scripture.

EXAMPLE:

"Be diligent to present yourself approved to God, a worker who does not need to be ashamed, rightly dividing the Word of truth." 2 Timothy 2:15 NKJV

I, [Chantell], will be diligent to present myself approved to God, a worker who does not need to be ashamed, rightly dividing the Word of truth.

Sometimes in order to add emphasis, I insert my full name:

I, [Chantell Mayes Cooley], will be diligent to present myself approved to God, a worker who does not need to be ashamed, rightly dividing the Word of truth.

Another example:

I, [Chantell Mayes Cooley] will rejoice always, pray continually, and give thanks in all circumstances; for this is God's will for my life in Christ Jesus. (1 Thessalonians 5:16-18)

Now, personalize these scriptures and confess them:

"If I [insert your name] abide in Him and His words abide in me, I will ask what I desire and it will be done for me." John 15:7 NKJV

"Let the message of Christ dwell in me [insert your name] and my family richly as we teach and admonish others with all wisdom through psalms, hymns and songs from the Spirit, singing to God with gratitude in our hearts."
(Colossians 3:16)

"I [insert your name] will flourish like a palm tree, I will grow like a cedar of Lebanon." (Psalm 92:12)

Let Your grace and favor increase upon me [insert your name]. (Esther 2:15-18)

Lord, You daily load me [insert your name] with benefits. (Psalm 68:19)

Father, give me [insert your name] the Spirit of wisdom and revelation, and let the eyes of my understanding be enlightened. (Ephesians 1:17-18 NKJV)

Let me [insert your name] understand heavenly things. (John 3:12)

I [insert your name] will arise, and shine, for my light has come, and the glory of the LORD rises upon me. (Isaiah 60:1)

WRITE AND PERSONALIZE YOUR CONFESSIONS

You can write your favorite scriptures and daily confessions here.

_____
_____
_____
_____
_____
_____
_____
_____
_____
_____
_____
_____
_____
_____
_____
_____
_____
_____
_____
_____
_____
_____

ALSO FROM
CHANTELL M. COOLEY

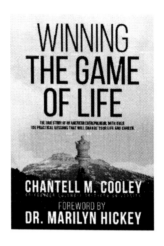

Winning The Game Of Life is inspired by the story of Chantell Cooley and her family, founders of Columbia Southern University (CSU). This highly motivational book challenges the reader to persevere through life's obstacles. Chantell shares over 100 practical life lessons from the game of basketball that molded her into a successful business woman.

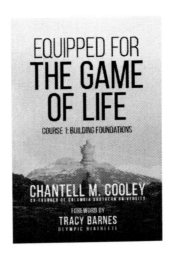

Equipped For The Game Of Lif*e* provides a strategic and systematic approach to mentoring. It will equip you with tools that are not part of the traditional college curricula, but are vital for the growth, development and success of the young adult.

Game of Life
Discussion Forum

To join other winners in discussing various topics from Chantell's books, you are invited to the Game of Life forum on Chantell's website.

www.ChantellMayesCooley.com

The Chantell Cooley Military Spouse Scholarship will cover up to $16,500 in one online degree program (associate, bachelor or master) at either Columbia Southern University or Waldorf University. For more information on criteria and how to apply visit Chantell's website.

www.ChantellMayesCooley.com

CHANTELL COOLEY LEADERSHIP
SCHOLARSHIP
FOR WOMEN

The Chantell Cooley Leadership Scholarship for Women provides financial assistance to young women seeking a residential degree at Waldorf University. These full tuition scholarships are awarded to women based on their leadership potential. For more information on criteria and how to apply visit Chantell's website.

www.ChantellMayesCooley.com